Children Learn What Grandparents Teach

Mavis Aldridge, Ph.D.

AuthorHouse™
1663 Liberty Drive
Bloomington, IN 47403
www.authorhouse.com
Phone: 1 (800) 839-8640

Published by AuthorHouse 02/23/2019

ISBN: 978-1-5462-7317-2(sc)
ISBN: 978-1-5462-7318-9 (e)

Print information available on the last page.

Any people depicted in stock imagery provided by Getty Images are models, and such images are being used for illustrative purposes only.
Certain stock imagery © Getty Images.

This book is printed on acid-free paper.

Because of the dynamic nature of the Internet, any web addresses or links contained in this book may have changed since publication and may no longer be valid. The views expressed in this work are solely those of the author and do not necessarily reflect the views of the publisher, and the publisher hereby disclaims any responsibility for them.

authorHOUSE®

CONTENTS

This book is dedicated:

to all the children of the world,

to the wonderful grandparents who help to raise them, and

to the dedicated teachers who academically enrich them.

ACKNOWLEDGEMENTS

This book is in large part the result of contributions
of proverbs from different sources.

First, I extend gratitude to friends, Alice and Norma, in whose conversations
I heard proverbs or wise sayings echoing those of my parents. Second, to my
siblings, Nina and Alma, who well remember those we have been taught by our
parents. Third, I am also very grateful to many residents at American House,
Wildwood, Florida, who generously shared many proverbs they learned and
passed on to their grandchildren. Among the grandparents who contributed
were: Doris, Don, Esther, Helen, Lucille, Pat, Patti, Nancy, Vito and Bette.

Finally, I cannot thank enough, Marie and Melissa, two former
teachers, who provided important feedback after devoting
their time and expertise to read the manuscript.

CHAPTER ONE – ART AND AN INVITATION

It was back to school in September, and the children in Miss Ellis's class were to turn in their summer projects. Jason was the first to submit his art work to his English teacher. "Here is my work, Miss Ellis! I finished it a week ago!" Jason said proudly.

"This looks beautiful, Jason. "Thanks, Miss Ellis. You are going to like it a lot. I just know it," as he walked off with a grin of satisfaction.

Just before dismissal, Miss Ellis said, "Children, I commend you for completing your projects. After studying all of them, I will have some comments on Monday."

Everyone in Miss Ellis's class was eager to hear her comments on the projects, especially Jason who believed his was the top prize. On the chalkboard, Miss Ellis listed the names of the children who had chosen the different categories: poetry, art, one-page essay, acrostic. She then presented positive comments on each and stated that she planned to create a display section for all. However, there was one that had no name. She asked that the student who did the art work with the bridge should come to her desk. It was 11-year old Robbie with the thick glasses and missing front teeth who went up to Miss Ellis's desk. "Robbie," said Miss Ellis, "you have in your art a bridge and a wall, and down in the corner are two children shaking hands. Did you do the art and what does it mean? Please tell the class about it."

"Yes, Miss, I drew it from something I hear Gramps say all the while, and NanaLou too. They say *'it is better to build bridges than walls.'* The two of them talk funny to me many times; sometimes I think they talk in doubles. They say one thing, but they mean something else, and they think I understand, Miss, but many times I have to scratch my head with my ten fingers, up and down, and pretend like I know what they mean. So I drew the bridge and the wall. I wasn't sure, but after a while I began to think it probably means that the bridge can make people cross over to another place, and like they connect, meet up or come together, but the wall is a barrier and just keeps them out. Like the two children I drew down in the corner, people should make peace, shake hands, and stop hurtin' each other. That is why I draw it like that, Miss."

"Robbie, write your name here at the corner, please" said Miss Ellis, "You have done very, very well. Class, what do you think?" All the children gave Robbie a round of applause, except Jason.

After school, when Gramps came to fetch Robbie, Miss Ellis told him about Robbie's project and the story he told the class. "You should be proud of your grandson, Mr. Jenkins. It seems you have caused Robbie to think about ideas, and that's good!"

"Well, Miss Ellis, thank you but you know, my wife, Louise, NanaLou as they call her, she is really the one. Every day she has more of these 'pearls of wisdom' as she calls them, for Robbie. She got them from her grandparents!"

"Hm! I get it," said Miss Ellis with a smile. "Would you and your wife come to our After-School Program and talk to the children about these 'pearls '? I think they would learn a lot from you. How about Wednesday at 3:30 p.m.?"

With a twinkle in his eye, a smile, a nod, and a wave of his hand, Mr. Jenkins said, "NanaLou and I will work it out."

CHAPTER TWO – GRANDPARENTS TEACH!

There was great anticipation among the twenty children in Miss Ellis's After-School Program. Grandpa Jenkins and NanaLou, Robbie's grandparents were ready to share their 'pearls of wisdom.' "Well children," Mr. Jenkins began, "what you heard from Robbie is just the tip of the iceberg. Do you know what that means? It means there is a whole lot more yet to be told, and we can't tell them all now. We will tell you a few today, and maybe, more some other time. Today, we will talk about how appearances can be different from what is real."

"That's true," NanaLou chimed in. "How many of you teased my Robbie and called him names because he doesn't look like the rest of you; he doesn't talk much, his eyeglasses are thick, he lost all his front teeth, and walks with a limp? Let me tell you, he comes home crying many days. You don't think he is any good, do you? Well, isn't that sad? Robbie is bright and intelligent! Miss Ellis thinks his art work is outstanding, and his explanation of it so good, that we are willing to come and share more of our ideas with you. So, don't judge people by how they look, but by who they really are as persons! Think more about ideas, you hear me, and you will be better for it! Looks can deceive, you know. Do you think that every man or woman dressed in an expensive business suit is an honest person, or every beggar is a thief? No!" Now, don't get me wrong. There are honest people in business and there are beggars who are honest!"

"That's true." Grandpa added, "Remember kids. Another way to say the same thing is, *'Never judge a book by its cover'*, and *'all that glitters is not gold'*!

"Exactly," chirped NanaLou. "Something can be beautiful on the outside, but not good on the inside, and it can be the other way around. You see, children, we are living in a world where there are some good people and some bad ones, and you need to be aware and alert."

Grandpa interrupted. "Why don't you remind them of the story of Cinderella?"

"Excellent," said NanaLou. "How many of you children read the story of Cinderella?" Many of the children raised their hands. "Good," she continued. "Remember the wicked stepmother who was always dressed up in her regal clothes and fancy jewelry, and how she and her daughters were cruel to Cinderella? Yet, Cinderella, who was the slave doing all the dirty work in the house, and dressed in ragged clothes, she treated them with kindness and respect. She believed in love and forgiveness. What a big difference! Do you see the difference children?"

"Yes ma'am!" came a loud response.

NanaLou concluded, "By the way, thank you all for not texting your friends on your cellphones during our discussion. Now, does anybody have anything they wish to say?"

Anna's hand shot up from the back. "I agree we should focus more on ideas that make us think about our world. Miss Ellis taught us about Stephen Hawking, a brilliant scientist who wrote books and taught about our universe. Even while he was weak and broken, and suffering from a crippling disease, and in a wheelchair, he still taught about the universe and black holes."

"You are quite right, child. That's a good point! You know Miss Ellis," said NanaLou, "I was a teacher in my much younger days and you seem to have a very alert class. We should do this again. As we said before, this is just the tip of the iceberg. Children, keep reading and learning as much as you can! Ideas make you think!"

In closing the session, Miss Ellis said, "Thank you for coming and sharing, Mr. and Mrs. Jenkins! Will we see you again next Wednesday?"

"We would like to come again," they replied. "Goodbye for now." With an approving look at the class, they sauntered out as Grandpa signaled, "Let's go, Robbie!"

CHAPTER THREE – A PROBLEM? WHAT PROBLEM?

Two days after this event Miss Ellis was summoned to the office of Mr. Johnson, the Principal of Eager Learners Elementary school. "Miss Ellis," he began in a stern, reprimanding voice, "we have been having several phone calls from several grandparents stating that they wish to attend your Wednesday After-School Program. Are you turning this school upside down? This is quite unusual, you know. Grandparents wanting to attend school, to be in your Fifth Grade class? What nonsense! Unheard of! Can you explain this? I won't have it! We do not teach grandparents at this school! Send them to a school for adults, that is where they belong! I am putting an end to this before it gets worse, and for that *you* would be responsible! Do you get that?"

Miss Ellis took a deep breath, then replied calmly, "Mr. Johnson, grandparents carry a lot of wisdom; they have rich experiences and life lessons which today's children need to learn; they have much to teach, and by dismissing them we may lose something valuable." After explaining what happened in her Program on Wednesday, she advised, "Mr. Johnson, *'let's not throw out the baby with the bathwater'*!"

"Now, now, just what do you mean by that crap?" Mr. Johnson slowly growled with his eyes flaring with anger.

Miss Ellis replied with a well controlled tone of voice, "Well, may I suggest this? Let's have these grandparents at least one more time; come and see for yourself what happens. You know, right now I am thinking about what little Robbie shared with his classmates, *'it is better to build bridges than walls!'* I invite you to join us on Wednesday after school."

Miss Ellis was not prepared for twelve more grandparents who arrived for her After School class. Benches from the cafeteria were brought in to provide extra seating. A tall, stocky gentleman was the first to speak.

"Miss Ellis, I am Jim Nelson and all of us here heard about little Robbie and his summer art project. We think you are doing a great job getting these children to think about ideas, and all of us here want to join with Gramps and NanaLou to tell more of these tales to the children. Some of us find ourselves separated from our grandchildren, and many of their parents don't have much time to spend with them. Why? Because life is causing many parents to work long, extra hours to earn enough just for the bare needs of food and clothing. Many barely have enough time for sleep and chores! Grandparents often fill the gap. Children need to understand what life is all about because too many young ones get drawn into addiction to violent games on social media, are disrespecting their elders, get seduced into drugs; some are failing in school, others falling into depression and alienating themselves from family and friends; others are idling and getting into mischief with the wrong crowd. We want to tell it like it is because we love and value all the beautiful and intelligent children in this school!" The principal had walked in, doubt written all over his frowning face, and had taken a seat just in time to hear everything Mr. Jim said.

"Mr. Jim," said Miss Ellis, "I am impressed by your words, thank you, sir. At least one afternoon for five weeks, we are trying to get the students to be more interested in thinking about ideas and how those ideas apply to their lives. We are glad you are here, and I am convinced that grandparents have a wealth of these ideas to share and create change. Please continue, Mr. Jim."

"Miss, there are others who wanted to come but couldn't make it today. But I was thinking what my grandparents would say about what is happening in our country and the world these days. What you started with the children, they would say, **'Little brooks make big rivers.'** Just like the Parkland youngsters who are marching in all the states to stop gun violence in schools, this could grow into something big. Who knows? The Youth movement began small but the actions grew because they realized that what happened was wrong and took action."

"And let's not forget, **'little strokes fell big oaks!'**" said another grandparent.

"Children," said Miss Ellie, "would anyone care to take a shot at what that means? Yes, Karen," gesturing to the student whose hand went up immediately.

"Miss, my grandma showed me an oak tree one day; it is huge, and she said if you keep chopping at it, after a while it will fall to the ground." Grandparents nodded in agreement. Karen further added, "Miss, that is how some people who should know better, or companies, or gangs who do bad things, they get punishment later. 'Cause there is law and the court, and a man called a judge will judge them and put them away. Then they would have to stop what they are doing, 'cause people kept talking and protesting." Much applause came from the group.

"Very, very good!" said another grandparent, taking a standing position. "What about the idea of taking steps to prevent a bad thing from getting worse? I was just thinking how my mother would say, *'a stitch in time saves nine'* and *'an ounce of prevention is worth a pound of cure.'*

At this point Mr. Johnson, the Principal attempted to speak when another grandparent interrupted, stood tall, and addressed the group. "I would advise everyone to listen to that one again and again!" Lifting his bandaged left leg high, he said, "Everybody, behold a big foot without its big toe! I now have to walk with a big stick or I will topple over big time!" The room filled with laughter.

His brother, Jimmy explained, "Everyone, hear this; that's because he did not do the stitch in time or that ounce of prevention thing when he got an infection! Ho! Ho! Ho! Oh, he thought he was Mr. Invincible alright, until the doctor who saw the badly infected toe said, 'Sorry Mister, this is your choice: either you lose the toe now, or lose the foot later!' My brother's eyes stared wide open in shock. 'You mean, you have… to c-c-cut off…m-my…' Mr. Invincible stammered, and before he could finish, the doctor nodded over and over. I was sorry for him, but he is my brother, and I love him!"

"In other words," said Mr. Johnson, the Principal, at last, "if you think something is not right, you must do something about it before it gets out of hand or you will lose control."

"That is a good explanation, sir," said the grandparent.

"To that I totally agree." Mr. Johnson added.

Miss Ellis was not sure what the Principal was driving at. Was he still objecting to the presence of the grandparents? Did he not grasp the contribution they are making? The children were listening to every word. One of the children in the front row raised his hand.

"Carlos, do you want to say something?" Miss Ellis asked.

"Yes, Miss. When my mother wanted to punish me for something I did wrong she would tell my father, *'if you don't crop it while it is a bud, one day it will require an ax.'* Is that the same thing, Miss?"

"Exactly! Holy cow! I don't believe this!" echoed one grandparent with raised eyebrows and excitement in his voice, "Yes, if you don't tackle the problem when it is small, it may need more time, money, and bigger effort later on to deal with it! This is getting more and more interesting, I can't believe this!"

"Can anybody give another example connected with what Carlos just said?" asked Miss Ellis.

"I can," said one of the women near the corner close to the Principal. "I want all of you to know there is something I will regret for the rest of my life. So, you young ones listen up! Value your life and the life of your classmates. Treat yourself and others with respect. We, your parents and grandparents, we love you and want to see you succeed and become great men and women! I nearly lost my grandson, Reuben, to drugs. I thought I was showing that I loved him when I gave him pocket money to buy things at school. Even though I was suspicious when his behavior changed, I did nothing to stop it, until I found out he was going out with friends, smoking pot; then they gave him what he was too young for. One visit to the hospital, and the doctors could not bring him back to his former self. He is now an invalid at seventeen! But my granddaughter, after her second fight with girls at school, her mother and I stopped all privileges until she came to her senses. We cropped it in the bud, before it required an ax! It never occurred again! Now, she is in college and taking courses to be a pilot!" Applause followed applause.

"That's right! That's what I believe!" said a firm, emphatic male voice. "I say it is better to **'Strike while the iron is hot,'** and **'don't put off until tomorrow, what should be done today**!' Turning to the grandmother who just spoke, he said, **'You cannot change anything about yesterday, but you can change everything about tomorrow'** and you did that with your granddaughter! Bless you!"

"Yes, I agree, we should tackle issues when the moment is right, especially with our children nowadays. If we don't, we may lose something or someone. We are living in a rapidly changing world, and it is hard on them!" added another. "If we are not teaching them what is right, then anybody will influence them with what is not for their good! We have to be alert! And that's all I have to say."

More comments and concerns were expressed on behalf of their grandchildren.

"Oh my, my Carlos!" said Miss Ellis, "thank you for sharing what your mother told you about the bud and the ax! It surely sparked a whole new conversation. Grandparents, what treasures you are! NanaLou and Grandpa Ed said our first effort was the tip of the iceberg, and it seems they were right. Give yourselves a loud applause! Now, I have a question, do you wish this program to continue?" There was a unanimous 'yes' by way of hoots, table banging, whistling, or raised hands, including a not-so-sure look from Mr. Johnson, the obstructing Principal. "Thank you, so we will meet again next Wednesday then," Miss Ellis continued. "Thanks for your contributions and thanks again for coming." Children and grandparents shook hands and smiled, while some did some hugging.

As everyone filed out of the room, Miss Ellis discreetly called Jason. At the same time, on his way out, with a nod and a grudging quarter smile, Mr. Johnson said, "Goodbye, Miss Ellis."

"Goodbye, Mr. Johnson," the teacher replied.

CHAPTER FOUR - A SPECIAL MOMENT

Sitting beside the young boy, Miss Ellis gently asked why he was absent last Wednesday.

"Because Miss Ellie, I was ashamed. I worked hard on my project and I was proud of it and believed that mine was the best, but you chose Robbie's art. I was feeling shame again 'cause I used to tease him and call him Mr. Ugly." At this time Jason began to cry.

"O.K. Jason, I am glad you shared that so honestly with me. But I didn't say your work was not good. Every child's work was good in its own way. You will have another chance to do your best or even better. You know, there is a saying which goes like this, **'When at first you don't succeed, try, try, try again!'** Be happy for Robbie; your chance will come one day! Now, are you going to continue calling Robbie bad names?"

"No Miss," said Jason with tears running down his face. "Tomorrow, I will tell him I am sorry."

"That's my boy!" said Miss Ellis. "Jason, may I have a hug?" as she dried his tears and they hugged each other. "You and I just built a bridge of peace, and broke down a wall of separation. Isn't that wonderful?" By this time, Jason was smiling.

That was a difficult, but rewarding day for Miss Ellis.

CHAPTER FIVE - THE ICEBERG
BEGINS TO MELT

Two days before the next After-School meeting, Miss Ellis was again summoned to the Principal's office. "What did I do now? Is this another rejection session," she pondered while on her way. "How much longer must my patience be tried by Mr. Johnson? I suppose now he is going to tell me I have been disobedient, I am giving the school a bad name, therefore I am fired, I am not the kind of teacher he wants in his school, therefore I should look for another job somewhere else. *'It never rains, but it pours'*. It is one problem after another with this man." Her thoughts were racing. "Perhaps I should abandon this whole idea. Angels of strength, come to my rescue." Much to her chagrin, Mr. Johnson greeted her at the door with a warm, welcoming smile.

"It seems word is getting around. Mr. Henderson, the County's Chief Construction Engineer called and asked if he could bring a few of his friends to the program on Wednesday. Of course, I told him we would be delighted."

"We?" queried Miss Ellis.

"Of course, I am on your side, remember?" said Mr. Johnson sheepishly.

Miss Ellis gazed at him in astonishment, and mumbled, "Thanks, but what a sudden turn of events; I thought you..."

"You will need a bigger room," the principal interrupted abruptly, "and I think the auditorium will be more suitable, so we will get that ready. Good day, Miss Ellis!" She returned to her classroom quite astounded.

"Children," she began, "give yourself a round of applause. On Wednesday, at our next meeting, we will meet in the auditorium because we will be having some special visitors, all because you have been such a stimulating class! Not just one of you, all of you together as a team! Clap your hands!" They did so joyfully.

At 3:30 p.m. on the third Wednesday of the program, over a hundred parents and grandparents were already seated in the school auditorium. Mr. Johnson, the Principal, greeted Mr. Henderson and his three friends and gave them front seats. At the microphone, Miss Ellis in a rousing voice said, "Welcome, everyone. Mr. Henderson, we are honored to have you, your friends, and all those attending our Fifth Grade After-School Program for the first time. This session, I believe will be another unforgettable hour and a half as we discuss ideas about the importance of having goals and reaching them. O.K. Who would like to start?"

Mr. Rick Henderson was the first to take the microphone. "I wish to congratulate Mr. Johnson and Miss Ellis for this unusual and stimulating program. Do you know how many children get into mischief after they leave school each day? Here, they are engaged in creative thinking! How fascinating! I wish to share this story about myself. At about ten years old when my grandfather saw me idling by just kicking ball, getting into fist fights, or not getting home for long periods, and neglecting school, he called me and introduced me to a ruler, showed me the use of a compass, introduced me to types of architecture, drawings, buildings, and bridges. One day when I complained that a task he gave me was too difficult and boring, he said, "Remember son, *'he who wants to eat honey must bear the sting of bees,'* and another time he quoted an abolitionist called Frederick Douglass who said, *'where there is no struggle, there is no progress.'* I never forgot that one! Once I went on strike because he was pushing me too hard. I wanted more playtime. I pouted and gave him black looks. I became my own boss and rebelled, doing my own thing, and acted like he was not important to me. You should see me one day with my little fists ready to punch this six-foot tall gentleman if he dared to come too close. I even imagined myself as swelling up like the Incredible Hulk ready to knock out his front teeth. To me he was a total jerk with all this nonsense and crazy double talk. Why can't old people talk right, sensible, and intelligent like me and other children I hang out with? I used to ask myself. 'It is so dumb, all these stupid things they say. Golly! They just drive you crazy!' After a few minutes, I shouted, "I want to get out of here, and work, and take care of myself! Then nobody will bother me!"

"Really? Now, that's a great plan!" he teased. "Have you heard that *'the bird who flies too fast will fly past its nest?'* Just so you know, the nest is the place of safety where the bird is secure, O.K?"

After that one, I gave him my back. A whole day passed by, then he asked gently, 'Tell me Rick, does it make sense *'to put the cart before the horse'*? Do you prefer to wallow in the dirty gutter, or do you want to breathe fresh air at the top of the hill and walk in the sunlight?"

"What? Excuse me! If you talking to me, can't you just talk English for once?" I yelled with disgust in my voice.

"Think about what I just said, Rick! When you have your answer, come and see me, I'll be waiting" he replied gently, oh so gently and lovingly. I felt like he gave me the harshest reprimand.

"For three long days I was angry and ignored and hated myself and my dear grandpa; I missed him so much but I didn't let on! *You never know the value of water until the well runs dry.'* Anyway, you know what? I realized he didn't yell at me, didn't beat me and lock me in a dark closet for hours, didn't call me names, or put me down by saying I had no ambition and would never come to anything, or ever bothered me again. All he did was give me food for thought and left me to my miserable, pitiful, confused self. What a lesson that was!" Mr. Henderson said, and with head bowed, he paused for at least ten seconds, shaking his head, and breathing heavily as he reminisced on his behavior. You could hear a pin drop in the auditorium.

Finally, one of the children, Marissa, rose abruptly on her feet, as the suspense was too much for her. She shouted, "Sir, what did you do?"

Mr. Henderson looked up suddenly and asked in surprise, "Young lady, what is your name?"

"Marissa, I mean my name is Marissa Mendez" she said. "I mean, did you run away to another relative, or to one of your friends' house, or sat for hours under a large tree, or hopped on a bus or train even when you didn't know where you were going?"

"No, Marissa, but I must admit I was very tempted, I mean, to run away. I look back now and I am glad I didn't. That wouldn't have solved my problem. For three nights I barely slept. All I could hear ringing in my ears were, 'sting of bees' and 'eat honey', 'struggle and progress', 'cart before the horse', 'gutter and sunlight' and 'bird flying past its nest'. What do you think I did Marissa? Take a guess."

"I think you were scared 'cause you didn't have any money for yourself, and you didn't know where you would end up, so you decided to feel the bee stings, and you did some struggling because you prefer the sunlight," responded Marissa.

"You are quite right! You grasped my feelings very well, Marissa. I felt the sting of hard work to graduate from college, but I have also tasted the honey of success. Today, I am not groveling and begging in a gutter or sleeping under a bridge like a homeless person. I realized that at my young age, to go out and work without even a good education, that would be putting plans for my life in the wrong order. Definitely, not a good idea. I would be *'putting the cart before the horse'*. I am now walking in the sunlight of my achievements as the Chief Engineer of this County," replied Mr. Henderson. "Do you know that many of the buildings, including the majestic Town Hall that you see in the Town Square were designed by me and constructed under my supervision, also the bridge one mile north of this school? I am proud to have been of service in the building up of this County!" All stood and applauded Mr. Henderson.

"One last thing I remember my grandpa said to me, **'You will never reach the top of the mountain if you keep looking at the same scene.'** If I had continued to pout and mope because the task grandpa gave me was too hard, I would never have known the view and feeling from the mountain of success from continuing in school. Today, when I look back now, as a grown man, some of the guys I used to hang out with, that's what they did. They kept looking at the same scene of no hope in the gutter; they didn't want to do homework, skipped school sometimes, yet they wanted to go to the next grade; some joined others who did bad things after school because they had no one to supervise them. Some had parents who had to work long hours to put food on the table; one parent went off and left the child with strangers and never came back; another was put in an orphanage. So, children, I will always love my grandfather. Love your parents and grandparents who are interested in you and love you, even when they seem to be a little rough sometimes and talk funny. Let's see some hands if you get that!"

"Yea!" echoed the children as some raised their hands and some whistled.

CHAPTER SIX – TWO GREAT MEN

Two of Mr. Henderson's friends, Frankie and Benjie, joined him at the microphone as if they were about to put on a performance. "Friends, now that these two good storytellers are here, I quit!" said Mr. Henderson laughing as he left to take his seat. Frankie began, "Let's hear it if you think our friend Rick learned a great lesson from his grandpa!" A roar went up from the audience. "We like to tell history stories. When Rick talked about looking at the same scene and never getting to the mountain top, quite a few people who made the world a better place came to my mind. I recalled a man called Mahatma Gandhi of India. He saw how his people were getting poorer and poorer under the British system and wanted to do something about it, but he believed in non-violence. Now, he could decide to just complain and mope all day, and let the injustice continue by looking at the same scene every day."

"But," and Benjie joined in. "he believed there was a mountain, a higher and more dignified way of life for him and his people, that is, self-rule for a nation without violence!"

"Correct," said Frankie, "and they reached that mountain of self-rule through persistent marches and protests. Gandhi suffered much, spent time in jail, and finally died for the cause, but the British finally yielded to give victory to the Indians. Yep**, 'no struggle, no progress'; 'no pain, no gain.'**

"But children, you also have to know this, that **'when you find your hand into the lion's mouth, you have to take time to pull it out!'** What do you think I mean by that?" asked Benjie.

"I know," said Harry, one of the Fifth Graders, raising his hand. "If you try to pull it out too fast, the lion would just chew up you and your hand real fast."

"You have a good point there, son," rejoined Frankie, "so it can't be a sudden thing. You have to study how to approach the creature. You need to have a plan how to deal with it! Raise hands if you heard of Martin Luther King and the Civil Rights Movement." All hands went up. "Excellent. Remember those many marches over many years? They pursued their goal until they went all the way to Washington until President Johnson finally had to sign the bill to end segregation. Always keep in mind also, that **_It is a long lane that has no turning!_** In other words, bad times cannot go on forever; something will change or improve. Now, both Gandhi and King served their fellowman and paid with their lives to achieve a right, something of great value, called freedom from injustice."

"And, just to make an important connection," added Benjie, "do you see how Gandhi and King never gave up? They continued to work for freedom from injustice. Isn't it marvelous, everyone? The same thing happened in the struggle for women to earn the right to vote! Two women, pioneers of the movement, Susan B. Anthony and Elizabeth Cady Stanton started with little streams until they became big rivers of supporters. The little strokes they made along the way finally fell the big oaks of prejudice. You see, at that time in the 1800's, women were not supposed to be equal to men! But they never gave up because voting is important! It took seventy years before women were given the right to vote!"

Frankie, who was nodding in agreement, eagerly added, "Some goals are easy to achieve, others are not, but what is important to you will require planning, patience, perseverance, and suffering. I am reminded of Nelson Mandela, another great hero, who, after 27 years in jail, became Prime Minister of South Africa and toppled apartheid, another unjust system. Wow! Now children, let's see you raise your hand, if you understand how that connects with any goal you set for yourself. Just think of people in sports, in music and entertainment, in inventions and politics, how they failed sometimes, but saw that failures were really lessons. They believed that 'if at first you don't succeed, try, try, try again!' All the children stood and raised their hands. Jason, who had heard that before from Miss Ellis, clapped and yelled the loudest, "Yea!"

As the two men took their places, Miss Ellis seemed impressed at what had just occurred as she went to the microphone. "I am certainly enjoying how your ideas relate to lessons we learn for life! The iceberg is really melting! We still have another half hour. Is there anyone…"

CHAPTER SEVEN – LESSONS AND A PLAN

Before she could finish her question, a shout came from the back, "I want to say something," said a grandmother in a wheelchair while a gentleman helped her to the front.

"Welcome," said Miss Ellis as she gave her the microphone.

"My name is Cecelia Ronalda, and this is my husband, Jeffrey, and we have been married forty-seven years!" A loud applause greeted their introduction. "Some of these sayings I heard from my grandparents too, and quite often, they helped us to think about how our actions affect our lives and the lives of others. In other words, actions have consequences, good or bad. You just talked about reaching goals and such things, and that's good. But, how about causes and the effects that come with time in reaching goals? Except the one about the bud and later the ax, I don't hear any of those."

"Well," said Miss Ellis, "we will be delighted to hear some of your wise sayings or proverbs. Thank you!" and returned to her seat while there was another applause.

"My father was an honest man, and for a while he couldn't understand why he kept losing in his business. Someone was stealing his merchandise, and he couldn't find the culprit. He kept saying, *'every day the bucket goes to the well, one day the bottom will fall out,'* and another one was, *'as you sow, so you will reap.'* The police set a trap, and who was the thief? His trusted long-time partner! The bottom of his bucket fell out alright, and what did he reap? Twelve years in jail!"

"But you can sow good and reap good, can't you?" asked Anita, as she stood, waving her hand from the children's section.

"Brilliant! Young lady, yes, you can!" quickly replied Mr. Jeffrey Ronalda. "Listen to this. My grandparents came from Pakistan long ago, so I keep up with some of the news. Not long ago, a fifteen-year old girl, Malala Yousafzai from Pakistan, was shot in the head by a violent group that is still there, called The Taliban. Why? Because she spoke and wrote for justice and equality on behalf of little girls and women who were denied education. I hope you realize how lucky you all are in this country! I am not in Pakistan, but I broke down and cried! Fortunately, doctors saved her life! What did she reap? Oh my! This young girl became famous, a great example for children around the world who are being denied an education. Not only that, she was the youngest person to receive such a high honor as the Nobel Peace Prize! Can you believe that? She could choose to hate in response, attack others in anger, bully, insult, and call other children hate names even though they are not responsible. No! She used her energies by continuing to sow seeds of good by raising funds. She even built a school for girls in Lebanon! Malala was just a kid! Can you believe that?" Then with his hands raised, he shouted, "Let's say hurray for all children who choose to follow the best in themselves!" That was followed by a thundering noise of standing applause. "Cecelia, why don't you tell them the story of that other little girl your parents raved about so much."

"You mean the happy little one who loved to write?" Cecelia asked.

"That's the one. Children, you are going to love this!" replied Jeffrey.

"Well," Cecilia began, "my grandparents came from Germany, and my grandma used to tell me a bedtime story that I loved very much. It was about Anne Frank, another young girl at thirteen, who through her diary, showed the world that you can still love and hope even when you are surrounded by hate and evil. She sowed good and reaped good, and that's real power! But that doesn't mean that life is all goody-goody all the time. Life has its ups and downs, because *'that's the way the ball bounces,'* Grandma would say. During World War II, this little girl kept a diary of her experiences while she and her Jewish family were in hiding under terrible circumstances in a small space in Amsterdam, Holland. This little girl's only weapons against fear and uncertainty, was her love for writing, a pen, and a diary she got as a birthday present." There was a pause, and the children were in rapt attention.

It was Jason again who broke the silence, "Did Anne Frank also get a prize?"

"Well yes, and no, not a Nobel Peace Prize," replied Cecelia. "You see, unfortunately, she died at fifteen in a concentration camp with millions of other children after the Nazis found the hiding place. But her father, Otto Frank, the only one in the family who survived the holocaust, found the diary and was amazed at the young girl's record of her impressions of life around her, even during winter. Her prize was that her book, The *Diary of a Young Girl,* published in 1947, also became a movie, and she became famous all over the world, even today! Every year, thousands visit the museum in Amsterdam to see the tiny space where her family hid from the Nazis. Listen to one of her quotations: 'I still believe, in spite of everything, that people are truly good at heart.'[1] She sowed her thoughts about everyday life in that hiding place and reaped world fame after her death. Remarkable! That's one of the reasons why Jeff and I decided that we should participate in this program, because I know there is a lot of division, anger and disrespect going on around our community. I also think this is a rich experience for all you children! You never know all the good that can come from this kind of communication for understanding! Thank you, Mr. Henderson, Miss Ellis, and Principal, Mr. Johnson. I feel enriched being here!"

Just as her husband was ready to wheel her back to her place in the audience, she whispered to him, he nodded, and then called out, "Miss Ellis, we have a suggestion for you." After their brief, private conversation, with a big smile on her face, Miss Ellis had an announcement for the audience.

"Everyone, today, we had another interesting session. When I heard the stories about those children, I realize that for our next gathering, we should begin to focus on some wise sayings about relationships. For now, we are closing with something special. The Ronaldas are inviting us to their fourth annual picnic to be held on Saturday before our last Wednesday afternoon in the series. It will be held on their beautiful lawn at 2:00 p.m., 27 Cypress Dale Avenue, three miles north of here, just across the bridge built by Mr. Henderson. They wish you to bring only your spirit of fun, joy, and friendship, and, don't forget, an empty stomach!" Everyone stood to give a hearty round of applause and gratitude to the Ronaldas. Grandparents and children exchanged smiles, handshakes, and hugs as they exited the auditorium.

Principal Johnson and County Chief Engineer Henderson, who were silent during the whole session met with Miss Ellis at the podium. "I have an idea," said Mr. Henderson. "This is an event that should be published in the county newspaper, *Better World News*." Without hesitation, Principal Johnson interjected "I like that, I agree, don't you Miss Ellis? At last our school will be getting the attention it has deserved for a long, long time!"

For a brief moment, Miss Ellis's jaw dropped, while her eyebrows were raised in disbelief. "Was this the comment of her frequent obstructionist?" she wondered to herself. "That's sounds like a good idea," Miss Ellis finally acquiesced. "But who will do the reporting?"

"Leave that to me," Mr. Henderson replied, as he shook their hands and departed with a smile.

CHAPTER EIGHT – A CHILD BECOMES MORE CURIOUS

The next day, Miss Ellis addressed her class. "Children, I am really proud of you for your listening, your participation, and your eagerness to learn something outside our regular classes. I saw none of you talking or disturbing anyone, or playing with cell phones or game pads. How many of you learned a lot yesterday?" All hands quickly went up, except one. "Lueling, you didn't learn anything?"

"Miss," she said timidly as she stood, "something is bothering me. What is 'tip of the iceberg'?"

"Oh my, thank you for asking that question! Would anyone like to explain?" asked Miss Ellis.

"Me Miss!" said Howard, seated in the back row. "I heard my grandpa who used to be in the Navy say it is a huge block of ice on the water."

"That is correct," replied Miss Ellis, "but there is more. The tip really means the top, the smallest part that is above the water. The largest part is under the surface of the ocean, and may not be visible and can be dangerous for ships. So, sometimes when grown-ups have a problem or a possibility, like our program, we may just grasp a little part of it. The larger portion is hidden and may finally show itself or melt. "Does that help, Lueling?" She nodded. "While we are on the subject," Miss Ellis continued, "you might as well hear about a special ship, that was skillfully built, called *The Titanic*. It was supposed to be unsinkable. It left Southampton port in England on April 10, 1912 for America. While crossing the Atlantic Ocean, it collided with a huge iceberg, was badly damaged, and many people perished! My grandmother's saying about that is**, 'up to the lip, the cup may slip.'** Just when an important event is expected to occur, something happens to prevent it.

Two boys began laughing heartily and pointing at each other distracting the other children.

"O.K. Jaime and Carlos, would you like to share what is so funny?" Miss Ellis demanded, slightly irritated.

Carlos stood trying to control himself. "Miss," he began, then there was another outburst of laughter. "Last Sunday, we were at a birthday party, and just when Jaime was ready to bite into his ice-cream cone, the scoop gave him a large pink moustache, then fell out and melted down his shirt, pants and shoes! Miss, he looked very funny. He began laughing, and other children began laughing with him! Then he put the cone on the top of his head, and twisted his lip to one corner of his mouth! Miss, he looked ridiculous! He was the perfect clown! Ha! Ha-aah!" Most of his classmates joined in his laughter.

Without joining in the laughter, Lueling's hand shot up again to settle her more serious issue. "Is what you said like what happened to The Challenger, Miss?" she asked.

"You mean 'up to the lip, the cup may slip,' yes! Where did you learn that?" Miss Ellie queried in surprise. Lueling held up a colorful book of stories about adventures into space which she had borrowed from the library. Ooh! A slight gasp came from some of the children. "Good for you, Lueling, thanks for sharing. I am really excited at how you children are reading and actively exploring metaphors and meaning through proverbs in language, and how it applies to your lives. Keep it up! At our next Wednesday After-School Program, we will talk about relationships; that's very important. For now, let's get into other lessons for the day."

CHAPTER NINE – AN UNUSUAL SESSION

At the next gathering, Principal Johnson was the first to arrive. The auditorium was filling up quickly and more chairs had to be brought in. As her students took their places, Miss Ellis was surprised that the crowd had increased so much with more parents and grandparents. She began feeling that this session was going to be unique but not quite sure how or why. At the microphone, she extended welcome to everyone, briefly reviewed the richness of the past sessions, and expressed anticipation that this session would be no less informative and unforgettable.

"This afternoon, in our discussion," she continued, "let's begin to talk about some wise sayings or proverbs that inform us about how we relate to each other, in good ways, and not so good ways, and how our behaviors affect each other. Our behaviors can drive us apart through hate and resentment, or bring us together in mutual respect and appreciation. Just a few moments ago, a shy grandmother informed me of two people who recently were hurling hurtful words at each other about previous actions of fraud against others. She lamented that they haven't realized that **'Those who have glasshouses should not throw stones!'** Then she made me think really hard when she asked, 'Does it make any sense, Miss Ellis, when **'the kettle calls the pot black?'** Is any one of them superior to or better than the other?'"

"In other words," Miss Ellis explained, "we are as good as our behaviors in our homes and communities, and the examples we pass on for young ones to imitate. In our interactions, we realize daily that character is very important for making our homes, schools, and communities the best environments they can be for healthy relationships. Yesterday, when I mentioned to my Mom what would be happening this afternoon, she immediately declared, "How wonderful! **'Birds of a feather flock together.'** I hope we have here a gathering of beautiful birds having the same interest for good."

A shout came from the audience, "We want to be good birds, people interested in doing good, like you said. We don't want to be like vultures destroying and picking at each other." Several feet tapped the floor in applause.

"Wow! Thank you. Well, in that case, standing here among you beautiful birds, I hope I am at least a tiny little one!" said Miss Ellis amid some laughter. "Let's explore that issue of who we are further, though. Let's communicate for better understanding about our actions and how they affect us. In other words, what wise sayings or proverbs reflect how we help or hurt each other? Let the comments begin!"

Before Miss Ellis finished her statement, a grandfather known as Rocky limped his way to the platform and stood beside her. "Before you take a seat Miss Ellis, I want you to meet some dudes from my social club," he said as he beckoned with his raised left arm. Three husky men with thick grey moustaches, dressed in jeans, leather half jackets, cowboy boots and hats, joined them and bowed respectfully to Miss Ellis.

"Are you going to sing, dance and play guitar?" she asked.

"Not exactly, Ma'am," one replied, "but we heard about your Wednesday afternoon gatherings and would like to contribute to your class some sayings which have helped to make us better men."

"Thank you Rocky, this is really cool! Gentlemen, I am delighted to meet you. Shout when you are ready! Everyone, we have a surprise!" Miss Ellis announced as she took her seat. Just then, the main door opened and Principal Johnson, County Engineer Mr. Henderson, made their entrance and sat at the back with a retinue of video camera men and reporters.

"Grandparents, children, and newcomers, I am Rocky, and these are my club friends, Raphael, FairElk, and Rasheed. We will be telling stories, so, sorry, this is important. Then he showed a sign, *NO SNORING ALOUD IS ALLOWED*! Raucous laughter could be heard from some in the room, while some teasing and finger-pointing occurred.

It was Raphael who began first. "Well folks, at age 68, I can tell you I learned many lessons from other people's experiences. One guy told me he had to leave his wife because almost every little thing was something for her to make a big fuss about, and all he just wanted was peace and quiet. If he didn't say where he was going when he left the house, or didn't put his dirty socks into the laundry bag, if their son didn't say goodbye before leaving for school, or put his dirty plate in the sink, a verbal storm rushed through the house shaking the rafters. One day he asked her, *'Why make such a mountain out of a molehill?'* As I listened more to my friend, I recalled what my grandma used to say about bullies, *'Empty kettles make the most noise.'* They feel neglected or in some cases not loved, so they are loud and often attack others to get attention.

FairElk said, "That is so true, and I have met quite a few! Shall I tell them the story we shared yesterday?" After getting the nod, FairElk asked, "Have you ever

24

heard that, **'He who digs a pit for others usually falls in'**? Yep! An officer I once knew in the police force made a false report of robbery on a youngster who was at the crime scene but the kid didn't even know there was a robbery. He arrived at the scene the same time as the police. No matter how he tried to explain his presence, he was arrested and sentenced to five years in jail. After three years, an investigation found the young man was wrongfully charged by the officer to fulfill his 'quota.' It was a case of **'One man's meat is another man's poison'**! But in this instance, the officer didn't enjoy his meat for long. The young man who was the victim of his poison was freed."

"The officer was stripped of his badge, pension and privileges, and sentenced to ten years in prison." Raphael added. "The same pit he dug for the young man, he fell in it. But there is more. The young man visited him in prison; the officer didn't even recognize him as the one to whom he caused so much pain, tears, and humiliation; he was just a number. The young man forgave him and wished him well. Isn't that something? That experience my friends, also explains how **'The ax forgets, but the cut log does not!'** That young man will never forget that cruelty. How we treat each other is important. Any violence, physical, verbal, or emotional, can cause wounds that even into old age are never healed! So, who we become is important! Character is important! And guess what? It turned out that the officer's father, who was also a police officer, neglected his son and treated poor people with disdain. It's like **'the chip never flies far from the block'!"** Raphael ended with a shout.

FairElk became passionate, and ended the story by emphasizing, "We need to remember that when parents and grandparents like us are good blocks, our children have a good chance to be good chips! I love to frequently ponder a famous Native American proverb," **We can only be what we give ourselves the power to be."**

"I agree, character is very important," Rasheed joined in. "But you should know, that the officer FairElk mentioned was reprimanded a few times, and if I am not mistaken, was suspended a few times. To be fair, his Supervisor, a well-respected Police Administrator, provided Refresher Courses for the officer to improve his skills, but that didn't seem to help. It is amazing how **'You can lead the horse to water but you can't force him to drink'!** That officer had the opportunity to serve like other good officers, but he didn't. It turned out that his off-duty hours were spent with other friends who made money by dishonest means, and there was even a competition among them. Anyone who reported the highest gain on a weekly basis, became 'hero'. My friends, what we do to others we do to ourselves! How long does it take for us to learn that **'if you lie down with dogs, you will get up with fleas?'** Well, he caught the fleas of his friends alright, and they bit him really, really bad! The latest news about him is that he became so frequently enraged in prison that he wounded two staff officers, so he was thrown into solitary confinement, a worse situation. His own lack of self-control took him **'out of the frying pan, into the fire.'** How sad! So what FairElk said makes a heck of a lot of sense that we give ourselves the power to be who we want to be, but I think we should make it the best of who we can be!"

"Beware of the company you keep." Rocky reminded his listeners. "I learned these lessons for my life and they still guide me about friends and my relationships! You bet! So Elk, Raphael, and Rasheed, and me, we always talk how these 'pearls of wisdom' play out across the board with family, friends, neighbors, strangers, people in the news, wherever. We have learned that life is beautiful, and we can make it so or not by our choices! In many cases, we choose how we want the ball of life to bounce! Children, everyone, if this makes any sense to you, show a hand!" Of course, several hands dangled above heads in the audience.

One grandmother stood up, fuming, shaking her fist, and pointing her right forefinger, sternly at the men, spoke in a loud, deep voice, as she stomped her way to the front. "I understand what you gentlemen have said, and it makes some sense, but sorry, I do not totally agree with everything!"

Everyone had turned around to see the new speaker of the sudden opposition. Miss Ellis invited her to come closer and use the microphone. By this time Rocky and his friends took their places wondering if they were in for a fight. Wow! Was there a disagreement? Did they say something that offended somebody? Is she one of the trouble-makers dividing the community? "Boys, get ready, we seem to have a big fight on our hands. You may need your boxing gloves!" Rocky warned.

"Tell us your name," Miss Ellis urged.

"My name is Rose, and I have five children, six grandchildren, and one on the way. I listened to Mr. Rocky and his friends, and it is like everything I heard from them was something on the negative side. Well, I just want to tell you that in this world, there are some positive sayings, and I drilled many of them into my young ones, and today, they are the better for it! You hear me? They are the better for it I tell you! I hope you understand that!"

Oops! Just as Rocky got up to defend himself and his friends, Principal Johnson and Chief Engineer Henderson hastily walked up to the podium. "Rose, thank you so much! This is exactly the break we have been waiting for! This is exciting! Oh my goodness! Am I excited!" By this time cameras were clicking, and one lady was scribbling furiously on a writing pad. "Miss Ellis, how many more sessions do we have?" asked Mr. Henderson.

"One. Next Wednesday will be the last in the series."

"Perfect," rejoined Mr. Henderson, then turned to Principal Johnson, "I am inviting you and Miss Ellis to hold the last session in the Town Hall in the Square. Let Rose present her positive expressions then. How is that?" Both bowed in gleeful agreement. "Audience, how is that?" A roar of handclaps provided the response. "Fantastic! We will meet then in the large community room of the Town Hall in The Square. These Wednesday meetings have been outstanding! That will be a fitting climax to this great community exercise."

"Just a moment, gentlemen," interrupted Miss Ellis. "Everyone, remember, the Ronaldas have invited us to their annual picnic on Saturday!"

"We haven't forgotten, Miss Ellis!" shouted one grandpa on his feet. "We are busy repairing our dancing feet by removing all the corns and callouses, shining our boots, and oiling our creaky joints!" Amid much laughter, he continued pointing his finger, "and here is a surprise! Eddie here promised he would clip his ten toe nails for the first time in nine months!" Eddie gave him a vigorous whack on his bottom. "Plus, we heard that Randy and his GrandBand will be there! My wife already took out her long, floral skirt and her red frilly blouse to go with it. She even started practicing her moves for the line dances with the broom as her partner!" There was more laughter.

"Great, that's the spirit! We are all set then for Saturday and Wednesday! Thanks folks! What a gathering!" said Miss Ellis. Another applause signaled closing and a lively departure.

CHAPTER TEN - THE PICNIC

At 3:00 p.m., the lawn of the home of the Ronalda's became the site of a festive occasion. Long tables dressed up with balloons and buntings caught the eye immediately, but the wide variety of dishes and platters of food stirred one's sense of smell and caused salivas to be drooling long before it was time to eat. Several tables and lawn chairs were quickly occupied. The Ronaldas and friends were busy welcoming the flow of party-goers. Randy and The GrandBand musicians were already setting the mood for comraderie. Some line dancers were already in action and having a great time showing off some inimitable, fast shifting steps. The gate of the home closed just as Miss Ellis and Principal Johnson walked in and were seated. At that time, the band was still playing John Lennon's *Imagine,* while a few couples slowly danced in another area.

Holding the microphone, Mr. Ronalda addressed the crowd. "Welcome, everyone, we are delighted to have you here. This day is truly special, because it is the first time at our annual picnic that we have the privilege of such a large turnout of our community, especially friends of our Wednesday gatherings! This picnic is our way of celebrating the remarkable participation and sharing in those enlightening sessions of conversations for understanding ourselves. Let's be the community which is helping to promote a better world. I believe this is becoming a model community!"

"Let's make it so and keep it so," a member of Mr. Ronalda's team shouted. "Yes, yes! I agree! Let's choose to make it so! There is so much good to cultivate and celebrate! We can be the best! Let the celebration begin!" It was music time again and a fast rhythm encouraged lines of people to dance into lines to have their plates filled by colorfully dressed servers.

Someone though was missing. Where are the children? Mr. Ronalda wanted to make sure that this time Jaime could lick a big ice-cream scoop that stayed in the cone and didn't jump and spill all over his shirt and shoes! Where are the children? Neither Miss Ellis nor Principal Johnson could explain their absence. At last, Miss Ellis saw Malik, who was hurrying to be with his Mom in the line. She asked, "Malik, did the other children in your class come to the party?"

Pointing yonder with his forefinger, Malik replied, "Yes, Miss. They are all over there in that huge treehouse whispering, laughing and moving around like bees with three of the grandparents. I was too late so they didn't let me in."

Both Miss Ellis and Mr. Ronalda knitted their eyebrows in suspicion, wondering if they should check it out. But Mr. Ronalda was really pretending. "What? In my treehouse? No, no! That's impossible! How could that be? You must be kidding? I don't believe it!" he said adamantly.

In less than fifteen minutes, the other nineteen children could be seen climbing down the steps of the treehouse gaily laughing and running towards the lawn to join the party already in full swing. Miss Ellis asked, "Children, where have you been? Mr. Ronalda and I became concerned that…"

"We're O.K. Miss, we were just busy playing some games," Jason interrupted with mischief written all over his face. The other children wore innocent looks and Miss Ellis realized it was useless asking any more questions. The three grandparents arrived and their serious faces gave a message.

Mr. Ronalda invited them, "O.K., you are the last line to be served. Jaime, hold on to your ice-cream this time!"

"Not a chance it will slip this time, sir!" said Jaime laughing.

Later, there was a big round of applause after everyone joined in singing and rocking with the band as they blurted out, *Try to Remember the kind of September, When life was slow and oh so mellow....*

The fun-filled afternoon closed with several comments of gratitude to the Ronaldas. Everyone felt special at such an enjoyable occasion for all the grandparents, parents, and children of the community to become a family of friends, as each made an effort towards meeting and respecting the other. Before the crowd began to disperse, the last comment came from Principal Johnson who gave the reminder of Wednesday's Town Hall event.

CHAPTER ELEVEN - CELEBRATION
OF A NEW COMMUNITY

On the following Wednesday at 3:30 p.m. the Town Hall became a site of much excitement. "What a gorgeous room! Look at those decorations and paintings! Holy Cow!" exclaimed one parent to another while pointing, "And those must be what they call chandeliers, right?"

"I guess so!" came the response from another who became interested in the glimmering lights.

Randy and The GrandBand was already on stage filling the room with sweet soothing music. Everything gave the impression that this last session was going to be another unusual, perhaps the most unusual one.

"What's happening," someone asked looking all around the hall with all two hundred and twenty seats already occupied.

"I have no idea, but I think something big is about to happen!" was the reply.

"Wait! Where are the children? Where are they going to sit?" One grandparent asked.

"Aren't the children supposed to be here like they used to, sitting in the front?" asked another with some anxiety. Some shrugged their shoulders, others continued singing and rocking, swaying right and left, and bonding, as the band played Neil Diamond's *Sweet Caroline*. It became loudest when, with the help of Randy's lead singer, they sang the words: *Hands touching hands, Reaching out, touchin 'me, touchin' you, Sweet Caroline, Good times never seemed so good, I've been inclined to believe they never would, Oh no, Oh no....Sweet Caroline...*

Through the back entrance a small group of distinguished visitors sneaked in and were given seats forming a new back row. They even joined in the singing and the swaying. Some members of the audience recognized them, but the fingers on the lips of one visitor stopped any cause for excitement.

Miss Ellis appeared from behind the stage curtains and broke the musical interlude. "Ladies and gentlemen, I applaud you for taking time to be here this afternoon. Our program today will be very different. You are in for a surprise! Remember last Wednesday, Rose Beckworth made us realize that although some sayings were good, she thought we should focus on more positive ones, and with some help, she found an interesting and unique way to teach them to us! Let me hear the applause you wish to give Rose and her Company!" All stood for a loud applause.

With a nod from Miss Ellis, the band began background music. One of the children, Akshara, immediately walked briskly in marching style from behind the stage curtain holding a banner, and at center front, made a brisk turn to the left. She was quickly followed by Josh with his banner, and at center marched to the right. Eight other children holding their banners high, followed, taking alternate positions, and eventually forming a straight line across. Starting with Akshara, and with Miss Ellis holding the microphone, each child loudly read a positive idiom with a cryptic meaning and an example.

1. **When one door closes another opens**…..you may lose one opportunity, but another or better chance comes later. For example, getting a job, or entrance to a special college, or winning an Olympic medal.

2. **Behind every dark cloud is a silver lining**: Difficulties may make things look hopeless, but better days will follow. A group of athletes and their coach were trapped in Thailand for two weeks in a deeply flooded cave. The chances for saving them became very slim, but a group of international Navy Seals divers undertook the almost impossible mission, and after nine to eleven hours, rescued them.

3. **The early bird catches the worm**….Doing something on time has a better chance for a good result than if it is delayed, for example, applying for a visa to enter a country before the quota closes.

4. **A bird in the hand is worth two in the bush**….what you have of value is better than risking it for what may look better, but you are not certain of. At the casino, keeping three thousand dollars for one's family needs is better than risking it at the casino believing that it may yield five or ten thousand more.

5. **The proof of the pudding is in the eating**….the quality of something is known only when you experience it, for example, when an elected representative carries out the promises he or she made to the voters before election.

6. **A star is best seen at night**…..the best in some people often comes out when courage is needed in a dark, threatening situation. Right after the 9/11 disaster in

New York City, First Responders Firemen went into the buildings trying to find survivors knowing that their lives were in terrible danger. Also, during World War II, Britain's Prime Minister Winston Churchill said, "We will never surrender," and joined with the Allies to defeat the German army and saved England from imminent attack.

7. *Cut your coat according to your cloth*…plan goals and activities according to the resources you have. If you only have money for a two-bedroom house, then don't try to build a mansion. Another way of thinking of that is, ***'Don't hang your basket higher than you can reach it!'*** Some people overspend especially during holidays, then Credit Card companies harass them for payments they can't afford!

8. *You cannot change the wind, but you can adjust your sails*….You may not be able to change a bad situation, but you can change how you react to it. Terry Fox, an 18-year-old Canadian athlete was diagnosed with bone cancer which resulted in an amputation of his right leg. He realized he would never be the athlete he once was. After receiving a prosthetic leg, and seeing so many children suffering from cancer, Terry Fox began the Marathon of Hope and ran over 3,000 miles to raise funds for cancer research. Terry died at age 18, but his world-wide legacy had raised over $750 million dollars for the cause.

9. *Where there is a will, there is a way*….in other words, 'winners find a way to make things work; losers find an excuse for why they don't work.' Using her Underground Railroad network, Harriet Tubman was determined to free 300 slaves from the South to find refuge in Canada over ten years and nineteen trips. She achieved this despite a heavy bounty on her head, and she never lost even one slave.

10. *As the tree is bent, so it will grow*. What happens in childhood can influence who the adult becomes. Madam Curie, who was a scientist and pioneer researcher on radioactivity, discovered radium and polonium. Today, these elements are important for use of the X-ray machine used in hospitals today. Who influenced her interest and taught her in childhood? Her father, who was an instructor of physics!

There was a drum roll from the band and a loud applause and whistling from the audience. Next, from Miss Ellis's class came the other ten children, who formed a line behind the first row. They held up banners as a reminder of the variety of wise sayings or proverbs and creative interaction that had occurred over the previous Wednesday afternoons.

"Holy Guacomole!" shouted a grandparent from the audience. As he made his way to the stage area, he continued "I can't help it. I just can't help it! I want to say something here. Miss Ellis, can you and the children sit for a minute, please?" "Sure, but be as brief as you can, please." While folding chairs were brought from back stage for Miss Ellis and the children, the grandparent began waving his hand to the audience, "Hello! Hello!" he shouted excitedly in a deep voice.

Everyone responded, "Hello! Hello!"

"Thank you! I couldn't contain myself any more after seeing this display from the children. Just yesterday, a friend of mine and I were talking. He was uncertain about a job he applied for. I said to him, *Where there's a will, there's a way.*" Then he said, "The salary is good, but it is the working conditions I don't think will be good." Somehow I remembered a saying I learnt in childhood, and told him exactly what I saw on the child's banner, *'You cannot direct the wind, but you can adjust your sails!'* Wow! In other words, you may not have control over your circumstances, but you can control how you react! Isn't this a coincidence? I am a veteran, and I told my friend about the *Invictus Games* that were held at Disney World in 2014. Do you know what 'Invictus' means, everybody? It really means 'invincible' or cannot be conquered. I explained to my friend that it was a most wondrous spectacle watching war veterans who returned home from war, maimed for life! Some lost both legs, others an arm, others an eye, or their hearing; some could only play from a wheelchair, but they were playing basketball, shooting hoops, competing, and winning! They could not replace what they had lost, but they were using to advantage what they had left to keep on living, encouraging, and cherishing each other! They had the will and they found the way to play and have fun! That, I believe, made them heroes again! I am Jack Dunning, a veteran, and a newcomer to this gathering. I am thrilled at what you are doing here! Thanks everyone for listening!" A roar went up from the audience, some standing, some whistling, some tapping feet on the floor, as he returned to his chair.

CHAPTER TWELVE – THE CLIMAX

Miss Ellis had the Fifth Graders collectively show their banners one more time before taking their seats. By this time, Colin, Susan, Josh, Maria, Raphael, Kenisha, Lueling, and Malik had gone backstage. Colin reappeared first with a banner which read: *WE BELIEVE THAT CHARACTER IS IMPORTANT.* The others joined him with separate banners which read: *Honesty, Responsibility, Respect, Generosity, Compassion, Humility, Integrity.* It was a five-minute silent declaration. At a cue from Miss Ellis, the eight children returned to their chairs, and the class rose, for their rendition of two of Red Grammer's songs with the help of Randy's GrandBand. The first was, *'Listen',* which celebrates oneness and diversity:

Listen, can you hear the sound/Of hearts beating all the world around/Down in the valley, out on the plain/Everywhere around the world a heartbeat sounds the same/ Black or white, red or tan/It's the heart of the family of man/Whoa beating away Whoa beating away/Whoa it's beating away...........

Randy had everyone joining in the haunting, repetitive chorus: *Oolala, Oolala. Oolala.....ohohohoh...etc.*

Then Robbie moved closer to the front holding a banner, which was his art project enlarged: A bridge and two children below shaking hands. Jason joined Robbie with a banner stating the meaning: *A bridge helps people to cross over, meet others, and connect in peace. A wall separates.*

The band began playing the second Red Grammer's song, *I think You're Wonderful.* Jason was the soloist, and his voice was rich and pure, arresting and penetrating. The audience was spellbound as they heard him singing: *I think you're wonderful/ When somebody says that to me/ I feel wonderful, as wonderful can be/It makes me want to say the same thing to somebody new/ And I'd like to say, I've been meaning to say/ I think you're wonderful too!*

Jason continued to sing the next stanza as the lead singer while the audience heartily joined in the chorus, *I think you're wonderful....too.* There was an extended standing ovation for the children, but especially the two boys. While the applause continued, Miss Ellis went backstage and returned with Rose, then some loud gasps were heard as they saw behind her, GrandpaEd and Nanalou!

Miss Ellis raised her hand for a brief pause, motioned the children to be seated and said, "Ladies and Gentlemen, meet Rose again! It was Rose who last Wednesday called our attention to some wise sayings which we were neglecting. She prepared the children with the positive proverbs for today's session! Please give Rose your heartiest applause!" All stood and applauded. "Keep standing. Rose we applaud your valuable contribution!" Rose bowed in acknowledgement.

Miss Ellis continued, "She had the generous assistance of two retired teachers, who came to our first session! It was their grandson, Robbie, whose art project was really the springboard for these gatherings by producing his summer project you have just seen. Please give them your heartiest applause! Rose, GrandpaEd and NanaLou, again, thank you!"

Motioning the audience to be seated, Miss Ellis continued, "We managed five sessions of creative and interactive communication in addition to an unforgettable picnic event. I had no idea, that in addition to providing such a festive afternoon last Saturday of food, music and dance, the Ronaldas secretly connived and sneaked with the Jenkins and Rose to use their beautiful treehouse for rehearsals. Please give the Ronaldas and the teachers a hearty applause!" Rose and GrandpaEd and NanaLou were beaming with pride. Then Miss Ellis asked all the contributors of proverbs in the audience to stand to be recognized. "Randy, please give us a drum roll!" after which she added, "By sharing experiences related to at least fifty-one proverbs or 'pearls of wisdom' as The Jenkins called them, and communicating for understanding, you have richly added to the potential for this community to reach its highest aspirations, and we thank you!" A rhythmic applause followed. "Please continue your applause for Randy and the members of his superb GrandBand!" Randy and his team bowed in grateful acknowledgement.

"All these events have generously helped to make our community more vibrant. Finally," said Miss Ellis, and after looking around in the audience, "I really.. thought… they would be here, but it seems….."

"We are here, Miss Ellis!" She spun around to see three people laughing as they emerged from behind the stage curtain where they secretly hid after leaving the back seats.

"Everyone, please be seated!" That was the voice of Schools Supervisor, Mrs. Graham. "I have been fully informed of the fantastic community spirit that has developed over the past six gatherings through the innovative interaction between Miss Ellis's Fifth Graders and grandparents. Miss Ellis, please come forward. Today, I present you with this Award for Creative Teaching."

"Thank you, but it was really not my...." Miss Ellis tried in vain to explain.

"Congratulations, Miss Ellis!" interrupted Mrs. Graham. "Principal Johnson, please come forward. Today, I present you this Award for establishing and supporting such a unique After-School Program. We need more of these Programs across the State! Congratulations!"

"Thank you, Mrs. Graham, I accept this Award on behalf of all the students and teachers of EagerLearners Elementary. Thank you!"

Mrs. Graham turned to Randy, the musician. "May we have a drum roll for these presentations?" and began applauding as a sign for the audience to follow. "There is more," she said raising her hand for silence. "Miss Ellis, I have a special Award for all your Fifth Graders. On this Award is listed all the names of the students in your class. They should be proud of themselves, and I hope they will continue to be a beacon for other children as creative and eager learners. I applaud them for their belief that character is important. Will Robbie whose art project sparked this remarkable series of events come forward?" Robbie, wearing his thick eyeglasses, limped nervously towards Mrs. Graham and accepted the Award, then turned and showed it to the class. "Congratulations to you, Robbie, and to your class! See, there is even a drawing of your proverb, 'It is better to build bridges than walls.' How true! Let's have another drum roll!" By this time Robbie was grinning, showed it to the audience, then turned around and gave the Class Award to Miss Ellis to place it in the classroom.

"I have another duty to perform," continued Mrs. Graham. "Everyone, as members of this community, be aware of the young ones who show special talents. During this afternoon's program, I heard a child's singing voice that I will never forget. It is a rare talent. Miss Ellis, please bring the student forward." Miss Ellis summoned Jason to join her near Mrs. Graham who asked "What is your name?"

Jason timidly answered, "My name is Jason McLaughlin."

"Jason, you have the potential to become an opera singer," said Mrs. Graham, "and I have the honor and authority to give you a scholarship to attend a Music School for your training, and you will have the opportunity to go very far. Remember Jason, *'If you aim for the sky, you may shoot the stars!'* Miss Ellis and your parents or grandparents will contact me for further instructions. Congratulations!"

"Thank you, Ma'am," said Jason, after receiving a handshake from Mrs. Graham, followed by a drum roll and standing ovation. Miss Ellis took Jason's hand, and while walking back to their places, Miss Ellis whispered to Jason, "Wow! Remember how you pouted because I didn't choose your project, and I told you that your chance would come? ***Every disappointment is for a good!***" "You were right, Miss, and I thank you!" replied Jason, still in mild shock.

Just then, firm footsteps could be heard coming up the aisle from the back. It was the tall commanding figure of Chief Engineer, Mr. Henderson. "Please be seated," he said with a gesture. "Hello! Hello! I am the one who was angry with my grandfather who gave me the choice to live in the gutter or breathe in the sunlight, remember?" "Oh yea, we remember alright!" shouted Jim Nelson. "You were lucky that you didn't decide to punch your grandpa with your teeny little boxing gloves! Ha! Ha! Ho! Ho!" he ended laughing boisterously inviting others to join him.

"How right you are, Jim! Perhaps you recall how I learned my lesson and was able to be of service to this Town Hall. Well, I am also very impressed by the way this community has come together because grandparents and children have been telling stories to explain how the meanings of proverbs play out in our lives. I am living testimony of how a child's life can be enriched by a loving and patient grandparent who told me some of those proverbs, but I was a rebellious little brat. I was a midget boxer with no training, but ready to show my first victim who is boss in the ring!" He walked to the first chair in the second row, and helped Grandpa Henderson to his feet. "Everyone, this is my loving grandpa who guided me into the sunlight, and showed me how to get to the top of the mountain. He represents all of you here." A loud applause, whistles and hoots greeted the ninety-year old gentleman.

Then, turning to the children on the stage, Grandpa Henderson said, "Children, be careful who you attempt to punch! That person may be the one who saves your life!" He turned to his grandson and teased, "And you! I remember that day very well; you were puffin' and huffin' and snortin' like a warrior ready for battle! Golly! You scared the daylights out of me, you know, especially when I saw those two boxing hands of yours! Truthfully, they reminded me of baby sponge balls! But good try, son!" He remarked with a grin and a twinkle in his eye as he slowly returned to his chair amid much laughter and a long standing ovation from the audience.

"And now for some final surprises," Mr. Henderson continued.

"More? Golly Wolly! This is the best day I have had for a long time!" uttered a loud voice. I love it! I think we should...."

Mr. Henderson interrupted, "First, a special edition of these events will be published in our local newspaper, *Better World News*. Be sure to get your copies with the write-ups and beautiful photos. Who knows, you may find a picture of yourself among them! Be sure to read the article about Mayor Hennessey's plans for improving the lives of parents. Second, after this event, as you leave the main door, each grandparent will receive a medal saying, *Gran, You are Wonderful*. Then raising his hand with a scroll, he said, "In consultation with the Mayor, we have been given a Proclamation stating that from now on, every year, this date, October 3ʳᵈ, will be celebrated in this County as Children and Grandparents Day!"

"Yea! Yea! Yea!" was the unanimous chorus, accompanied by whistling, and feet stomping, which came from almost everyone. A drum roll accompanied the chorus.

Miss Ellis came to the front of the stage. "Thank you so much Mr. Henderson for such generosity. To bring this program to a close, Randy, can you and your Band once more help us to tell each other, *'I Think You're Wonderful'*? Jason, please lead us again!"

Jason was more than ready; all joined him in the chorus before and after his solo verse.

I think you're wonderful, When somebody says that to me, I feel wonderful, As wonderful can be; It makes me want to say, the same thing to somebody new, And by the way, I've been meaning to say, I think you're wonderful too.

If we practice this phrase in the most stylish way, Find something special in someone each day, We'll impact this world, one heart at a time, It all starts by saying this one simple line......Chorus

Handshakes, hugs, laughter, comments of congratulations could be seen and heard as the audience began leaving Mr. Henderson's famous Town Hall, in the city of Cordial, Bonvita County, Idyllwood, Newland.

CHILDREN LEARN
WHAT
GRANDPARENTS TEACH

By

Mavis Aldridge, Ph.D.

REFERENCES

Boyer, Crispin. *The Book of Heroes: Tales of History's Most Daring Dudes*. Scholastic Press, 2016.

Drimmer, Stephanie Warren. (p. 124). *The Book of Heroines: Tales of History's Gutsiest Gals*. National Geographic Kids, Washington, D.C., 2016.

ABOUT THE AUTHOR

Mavis Aldridge grew up in rural Jamaica, West Indies, where intergenerational relationships were part of her growth process. In her mature years, she began to deeply appreciate and recognize the value of that aspect of her life after migrating to the United States, where for many years she was separated from relatives.

She is an author, retired educator and administrator, whose teaching career spanned grades from Kindergarten to College. One highlight of her experiences relates to the numerous rich and memorable moments she spent with children in the elementary grades. As a result, she always had a fervent desire to write a book dedicated to children and the grandparents who influenced them in many ways.

Dr. Aldridge hopes that the book will serve as a catalyst for much sharing and reunions among children, relatives, and friends. She is happy and proud that she has finally fulfilled her long held desire to use this book as the medium for celebrating the innate genius of the children of the world.

Printed in the United States
By Bookmasters